The Price of Memory

# THE PRICE OF MEMORY
## AFTER THE TSUNAMI

MILDRED KICONCO BARYA

MALLORY

Published by
Mallory Publishing,
Aylesbeare Common Business Park,
Exmouth Road,
Aylesbeare,
Devon,
EX5 2DG,
England

For a complete list of titles, visit
http://www.mallorypublishing.co.uk
e-mail: admin@mallorypublishing.co.uk

First published 2006 by Mallory Publishing
Copyright © Mildred Kiconco Barya 2006
Cover photograph of the author
© Mildred Kiconco Barya 2006

**ISBN 1 85657 102 5**

Cover design © Mallory International Limited 2006

All rights reserved. No part of this publication may be reproduced, stored in a retrieval system, or transmitted in any form or by any means, electronic, mechanical, photocopying, recording or otherwise, without the prior permission of the publishers.

## Mallory New African Writing
An Introduction to the Series

All of us at Mallory International are delighted to have the opportunity to launch a new fiction series, incorporating innovative work from young writers in Africa, in conjunction with the British Council. *New African Writing* features unpublished works, some of it by previously unpublished authors.

Mallory International is primarily a bookseller, and most of our business is in Africa, so we have a commitment to African education and culture, and publishing gives us an opportunity both to publish new works and (through our *Classic African Writing* series) to improve the availability of past African classics which have been allowed to go out of print.

I need to record our thanks to Richard Weyers, Director of the British Council in Uganda. *New African Writing* was his idea, and he describes overleaf how it came about. I think it is the kind of initiative which shows the British Council at its best.

We are interested in developing both parts of our list, and if you know of (or have written) an important book now out of print – or if you are a new author without a publisher, please get in touch. No promises, but we will certainly have a look. Contact details are on our website, at http://www.malloryint.co.uk

*Julian Hardinge*
*February, 2006*

## Foreword

It's a special kind of privilege to be able to help others realise their dreams. Publishers regularly fulfil that role and in this case the British Council too, through this happy partnership with Mallory International. *New AfricanWriting* is an attempt to bring more of the incredibly vibrant writing coming out of Africa to a wider public. It is based on a very successful programme of creative writing called *Crossing Borders*. Since 2001 nearly 200 talented young writers from Cameroon, Ghana, Kenya, Malawi, Nigeria, South Africa, Uganda and Zimbabwe have participated in this distance learning creative writing programme delivered by the British Council in collaboration with the University of Lancaster in the UK and many African partners. *Crossing Borders* began in Uganda and it is therefore only appropriate that this series should begin with some of the best new writing coming out of Uganda.

For more information about Crossing Borders please see www.crossingborders-africanwriting.org

The British Council is the United Kingdom's international organisation for educational opportunities and cultural relations. It connects people worldwide with learning opportunities and creative ideas from the UK and builds lasting relationships between the UK and other countries.

*Richard Weyers*
*Director*
*British Council Uganda*

# Dedication

To Ojeya,
Daughter of dance
We were so little together,
But we loved much.

# Contents

| | |
|---|---|
| **Poems of Pleasure and Pain** | **15** |
| | |
| Dear Universe | 17 |
| Wastelands | 18 |
| Hot Springs of Lake Bogoria | 20 |
| Memory Eyes | 21 |
| That Certain Smile | 23 |
| The Lesson of Love | 25 |
| Africa Re-disappointed | 26 |
| Burning Fingers | 27 |
| Mathematically Proven Love | 29 |
| Don't You Remember? | 30 |
| The Contest | 32 |
| The Blind | 33 |
| Chase | 34 |
| Reminiscence | 35 |
| Beyond | 36 |
| Country Mirage | 37 |
| Children | 38 |
| Maybe | 39 |
| Silhouettes | 40 |
| Dreams | 41 |
| Remains of Sweetness | 42 |
| The Island | 43 |
| Resilience | 44 |

**Poems of Weakness and Strength**     47

| | |
|---|---:|
| Come Away | 49 |
| Love was a Smile | 50 |
| You and Me | 51 |
| Love, Faith and Hope | 52 |
| If That Isn't Love | 53 |
| Behind the Stone | 54 |
| This Man | 55 |
| Upon a Rock Viewing Bujagali Falls | 57 |
| Colours | 58 |
| Love | 60 |
| The Cross | 61 |
| Another Chance | 62 |
| Perhaps | 64 |
| Biologically Complicated | 65 |
| Solo Blues | 66 |
| They Asked Too Many Questions | 67 |
| Gifts of who we are | 68 |
| After the Tsunami | 69 |
| Unspoken | 71 |
| Poem for Betty Kituyi | 72 |
| Will We? | 73 |
| A Cup of Coffee | 74 |

## Poems of Identity and Renunciation 77

| | |
|---|---|
| I Know who You Are | 79 |
| I Will Be | 80 |
| You Tell Us | 81 |
| I Wasn't Born a Woman | 82 |
| That Old Man on a Bench in a Park | 84 |
| Some Men Find it Hard to Complete | 85 |
| Forgotten | 87 |
| At the Inauguration of a Pauper | 88 |
| Child of the Universe | 89 |
| Life | 90 |
| Bust Cisterns | 91 |
| Borderless Africa | 93 |
| Baggage | 94 |
| Gaza | 95 |
| Do not Look for Me Among the Broken Pots | 96 |
| Becoming gods | 97 |
| Oneness | 98 |
| Picture Bazaar | 99 |

# Poems of Pleasure and Pain

**Dear Universe**

Were you always fair
Truly without fault
As time began?

Were you without woe
And common foe
Till Satan became?

Did you dwell in bliss
And perfect peace
Before the serpent?

How could you a garden so pure
Listen to evil's lure
And give in?

Did you ever think about the price
Once or twice
That your fall would cost?

\*

## Wastelands

I've been to the wastelands,
Again.
Empty wine bottles,
Coca-Cola bottle tops,
I exhumed the remains
As if to rediscover my friends there.
Tears threaten,
I recall the years eaten by locusts
The palmist reading the future
Our eyes to the stars.

Memory is nothing but a collapsed heap
And time so false.

A young boy passing by watches me
Does he know why I am here?

I touch my forehead
A cup of coffee would do me good
Coffee days used to be celestial.
Restlessness puts his arms around me
Perhaps a walk to the cathedral,
To restore the me to my maker
Life feels dry like a severed foliage leaf
It wasn't like this in the beginning
I remember a rich collection-
A basket of promises

Drawers of dreams
A heart full of music
Soul sated with love
And wings to fly so high…
Becoming gods.

I listen to my heart,
Cracking
I rouse the vestiges for the last time
The life within must not die

I stand on the ruins
Not sorry for the past,
I would live it again for a lost touch,
Life and love,
And a cup of good coffee,
In these wastelands.

*

## Hot Springs of Lake Bogoria

A fountainhead
Spits fire
For earth's children.

We watch in wonder
And boil our eggs wrapped in handkerchiefs
In the belly of hot-springs.

A minute later,
We are shelling the eggs
The coffee is creamy sweet.

We've become child-like,
Boiling eggs and drinking coffee
In the pit of Lake Bogoria.

*

**Memory Eyes**

In the deep of his eyes,
I saw my own reflection
My heart rose like a wave
My mind swung on the flying trapeze
I loved him,
I held him.

I opened my eyes

I don't know how long he was gone

I stooped
To pick splinters of my heart
The stab of rejection
Holed through my mind,
Numbing me.

My soul waited for his return

Heels of time
Promised healing

I don't know how long I waited

I closed my eyes.

I was the mourning woman seated in the moon,

Sluicing with the wind
At midnight I smiled alone
The streetlights died,
Another day was born.

I shed off memory like a cloak
And evolved with the sun.

My life re-began.

*

**That Certain Smile**

That certain smile
Seemingly saying;
Do not mind the cobwebs in my house
Come in and we'll dwell together
Mirror and object.

That certain smile
Seemingly saying;
I see far,
The song in your laughter
Is the music of my age.

That certain smile
Seemingly saying;
Do not mind the gaps in my teeth
They are windows of yester youth
I am your crystal ball.

That certain smile
Seemingly saying;
I do not mind your prattle
Relish your fond years
It's a rich heritage.

That certain smile
Seemingly saying;
I forgive you my brother, my sister

Life is still a maiden lamb
And the he-goats are in the pen.

That certain smile
Seemingly saying;
You may now go
So long as we love
We continue to live.

*

## The Lesson of Love

We talked and talked,
And feared the sun might turn into sawdust
We held hands until our hearts melted
Until our eyes burned with sweet-ache
The ash of our past was swept off,
By winds of our present.
We picked our future like pocket-handkerchiefs,
Arranged in rows and packed into software
Marked 'Re-written.'
You Me.

We talked and talked,
And feared the moon might start to bleed
Having watched us so long without a blink.
On each we rested,
So same were our yester-lives
Alike here and now.

We talked and talked,
And feared the stars might fall down
Having witnessed our being,
As we chronicled the lesson of love.

*

## Africa Re-disappointed

When we were young,
It was easy to dream:
We carried galaxies in the laughter of our eyes,
And a rainbow in the small size of our pant-pockets.
We ate the tropical sun for breakfast,
And drunk the evening breeze for supper.
When we took a stroll to the Lake beaches,
The waters turned green at our command.
Now,
We stir the cinders of yesterday,
For remains of today
Memory like wake does not leave us alone
In the deadness of the night,
We are shaken out of sleep
We stare at the aborted dreams,
Hope miscarried,
Shall we sit, shall we stand?
Shall we walk, shall we run?
We send the eye to peer into the future
We are shocked to discover the future came…
What can we do now?
There's a hole in our trousers' pockets,
The rainbow is lost
There is a worm in the night sky,
Eating away the stars
And the sun we ate in plenty,
Has turned our breath sour.

\*

## Burning Fingers

We've been silent
Absorbed in hardened selves
Granite aloofness.
Time trickles like a drizzle,
There's plenty of it, we assume
None of us moves from seats of indifference.
We slip out of our bodies,
Unresponsive.
By the time we lift up our chins
To look through windows of our soul,
We are quite spent:
Our heads are a silvery white like mercury
The once firm limbs give way to feeble knees
The tight sinews to our frame stretch like chewing gum
Hands hang limp to our sides like a pair of old socks
Our eyes are buried deep in the forehead
In a lethargic monotone we speak
There's no one to love us, to hold us
To grieve our deadness before death
Without staff we are not ourselves
We cannot poke at the stones in our way.
Stars close in sleep:
'Husband mine,' it's a whisper
'Dear wife,' he says
A smile appears,
A tear shimmers,
We should have known

Years consumed in cold anger
Burning fingers
We've regained ourselves too late
We grin,
Beaming off our toothless-ness
And moaning salty tears.

*

## Mathematically Proven Love

If you get 12 calls a day,
6 of them are from Zaveda
If you get 52 calls in 52 weeks,
26 of them are from Zaveda
If you get 8,760 calls in 8,760 hours,
4,380 are from Zaveda
If you get 525,600 calls in 525,600 minutes,
262,800 are from Zaveda
If you get 31,536,000 calls in 31,536,000 seconds,
15,768,000 are from Zaveda
If you get 365 calls in a year,
More than half the calls are from Zaveda.
And if no call comes to you,
In a second, a minute, an hour, a day, a week,
        a month, a year,
You'll know for sure,
Zaveda is dead.

\*

## Don't You Remember?

Don't you remember,
When we sat in your compound
Eating raw salted mangoes
Like baby monkeys?

Don't you remember,
When we squat on the veranda
Nibbling sugar cane
Till our gums bled?

Tell me you remember,
When we plucked jackfruit
And your eyes held mine
In a tight embrace.

Surely you remember,
When we sipped the evening's breeze
And counted eternity,
On a single breath.

You do remember,
When we computed the stars
And the man in the moon
Smiled down at us.

Say you remember,
When we sat in the cinema hall

Eating popcorn
And never actually watched the pictures!

You memory-eroded one!
If surely you don't remember,
When we coiled on your sofa
And read poetry loud,
Let's give our present a new name
And call our lives a lying game
And when you read this verse
Let it be nothing but words
Oh, forgetful you!

\*

## The Contest

Our hands hug empty cups
Littered on the table
We do not rise to go home
We stare at the espresso residues
And puff billows of cigarette smoke into the night air.
We place our orders,
Beers colder than a freezer compartment
And the guinness bitter than sour honey
The universe becomes a dot of chalk on board
Lenses of gloom capture cynical mindsets
And magnify the fallen leaves;
We are truly nothing but animated clay
Rising dust,
Our energies dry
We cannot tell a humble cry from a desperate plea
Loneliness,
Callousness,
Restlessness,
What happened to the person called me, you, us?
Tired of hope,
Dreams wither
We hang between breath and lifelessness
And the divine in the ordinary does not give up
It opens a world wider than glory,
And faith wins.

*

**The Blind**

She walked him across the sea-blue sky,
His heart never to melt
She skated him on a wide cumulus,
His heart remained a clod.

She floated him on the serene sea,
His eyes never to see,
She rafted him to the shore-
His eyes remained sightless.

\*

### Chase

You kept the master spade-
I held the other aces
Both of us to win.

We knew the screens, the sites,
Pages unknown to others
We logged in, signed in.

Oh, the game we played
Then you gave away the password,
The chase!

*

## Reminiscence

She remembers,
Oh, she remembers:
Before he went to the army
He came into the room
Cupped her cheeks in gentle hands

'Be nice,' he said,
And kissed her.

He gave her a gift of a blue-cover notebook

Words turn hollow like bamboo stem.

A score of years gone,
He walks into the room.
She's been writing to survive reality
He opens the pages
Fond lines spring at him
He does not recollect
Memory lies in a trench.

The longing…
She's been living on borrowed time
    He's hanging on a short circuit fuse.
    Hope lies
    She cries into the notebook
              He does not remember.
\*

## Beyond

Where comes this speech
In the present age?
The words to the past
Signal a root dead,
A shoot that's not smiled to the sun,
A tender stem wrung.

Who's trampled on the plant
And stopped the seed from sprouting?

The mind in careful suspension,
Sees no time beyond now.
Hurt is inch by inch.
The state of confusion
Lingers.

How did we get it wrong?

But how were we to know the sun shines
If we never knew light?
How would we tell the smell of rain
Without sniffing the damp soil?

Nagging doubt tugs at the heart
In the coming years,
Will another seed drop and grow,
Will it be watered and nurtured
To blossom without weeds-
Or will it fall upon dead soils?
*

**Country Mirage**

A valley dam
A lake of sand
And the people cry
Water!
They go away.

\*

**Children**

Wolves
Guard children of men.

Computer games and videos,
Their siblings.

The unwanted,
End in garbage heaps.

Smiling faces and pouting lips
Never to see.

*

## Maybe

Maybe,
The hollow-eyed children will run into the house
Once with prancing steps
And announce Papa is back.

Maybe,
The dove will yet bear a sacred branch
To declare the warlords return.

Maybe,
Before my ears have gone deaf
I shall hear the trombone
Sounding the end of the plague.

Maybe,
I shall stare at the sun going to sleep
The hyenas and jackals
Fighting over bones of the dead.

Maybe,
I shall simply lie here
And let my skeleton carry the tale
'She died of exhaustion'.

*

**Silhouettes**

From the woods,
I see them
Countless figures
Etched against a yellow disappearing sun.

I must paint them
And give them dreams.

I spread the canvas
And schemes of luminous colours.

Darkness covers the plateau
Vision fails.

The silent tales fresh from war vanish
All that remains:
Are bleeding stumps of trees
And aborted children.

*

**Dreams**

Do dreams decay
That fail to flower?
Do they wither,
Expire,
That tire to bloom?

Heavy dreams that miscarry
Do they retreat to mummies chamber
Do they conceive again?

Wombs of dreams
Whose children are shrivelled
Do they spring with fruit again
Green leaves to sprout?

Dreams with a deathly pallor
Refusing yet to die
Languid dreams in minds sickbay
Do they wane
Do they wilt
Forever dreams?

*

**Remains of Sweetness**

The lamplight dies
Restless feet comb through dirty alleyways
Crashing cigarette butts
Eyes search for a place to lay down emptiness
Mosquitoes fill the night with biting songs
There's a call from London
Two souls embracing wake
Looking for grains of sugar
To sweeten the espresso
Lasting bitterness on the tongue.

*

**The Island**

The feeling is strong
Like losing something very familiar,
Like loving.

Zanzibar,
Will you dream of me?
Would you dream of me?

*

**Resilience**

Yesterday,
We loved.

Today we did the same,
Even when our hearts
Were crushed and pounded to powder.

Tomorrow,
At the sight of sunbeam
We shall love again.

*

# Poems of Weakness and Strength

**Come Away**

Darlin'
Come away when the trees are young,
We'll share the twilight
And sip the evening breeze
With the smile of the half moon.

Come away, love
We'll sing with the wind
And make dusk our transition
To the oneness of our being.

Come to me, please
We'll drink the sap of dawn
With the dew caressing our feet
And watch the grin of the rising sun.

Darlin'
Come away, now
For when the last tree dies,
We die.

*

**Love was a Smile**

You never told me
Love was a smile
I went in quest,
In dedicated pursuit
I sought the sage,
Love remained a riddle.

You never told me,
The answer was within me.
You let me wonder,
Left me to wander.

And love was a smile!
Had I known earlier,
So much time,
So much value,
So much self,
Would not have been spent!

*

**You and Me**

From the beginning,
I thought you so mean
Couldn't lead to a garden of geranium
But picked a little moss.

Thought it wouldn't last,
You were you,
I was me,
And we remain.

It has worked,
I know why-
It was from the rock
That we began.

*

## Love, Faith and Hope

Love within
Stirs,
Outwardly
Flows.

Faith inside
Walks
Outside
Leaps

And hope
Lingers,
Dream-like
Lives.

*

## If That Isn't Love

He tells me,
I'm the iris of his eye,
The lamb of his meadow,
The love of his bosom,
Peculiar.

He clothes me in lilac and purple
Raises the sceptre for me,
To enter his chamber.

He tells me,
I am fearfully and wonderfully made
Hewn from the ageless rock
Fashioned by the priceless romancer
Designed before time began.

If that isn't love,
Then, the moon is simply cheese
And the stars are mere popcorn in the sky
The clouds are but thick smoke,
And the lilies in the valley
Nothing but tall worms,

If His isn't love.

*

**Behind the Stone**

They laid him there,
Behind a stone.
The stone moved
For right of entry.
Today I walked through the cemetery
To read inscriptions -
'Great works she brought upon earth,'
'Infinite wisdom lies here,'
'Adorable father,'
'Loving mother,'
'Beloved child,'
'Loyal citizen'
But none to match the empty tomb
The legacy:
Born before the world began
Died to live, rose to immortality
He who was and is,
The meaning behind the stone.

*

**This Man**

This man,
I doubt if he ever went to McDonalds,
Or drank Starbucks coffee and advertised for coke.
I wonder if he ever took chocolate in the cafes
Did he taste pork ribs, beef steak and chicken wings?
Did he even hang out in the clubs?

This man,
Was he ever on the World Bank funding committee?
Or one to write a report for International Monetary Fund?
Did he chair any political analyst symposium?
Or move a referendum, amend the constitution
The Banana Republic upon his head?
Was he an expert in bomb handling and terrorist tracking?
Clearing, forwarding and deporting?

Perhaps he played in the BEATLES' band
Or sang with ABBA?
Shook his pelvis like Elvis Presley!

He was well known, unknown
Not to be found with illustrious connection gadgets
Did he even know how to use the internet, or create a website?

Was he ever wired and powered for sound?
Yet,
He reached hearts and minds
To the great divide of the bone marrow.

He went by unnoticed, noticed
He was eloquent,
And no sophistication was found in his speech
Few understood him;
Understood him not,
His truth, his language;
His folkloric parables and metaphors,
Touching earth and sky.

No roads or stadiums are named after him,
Save the highway
I am told he lives before all things and in all things
The source of continuation
He went to burial grounds and barren fields
And released fountains of life.

The world knows this man
Does not know,
Some have seen him
With their hands they've touched him
Still waiting to deliver
The world's ransom.

\*

## Upon a Rock Viewing Bujagali Falls

There,
On the rock,
Was Mr Dreadlock.
On the shore,
Sat Mr. Fisherman
Hook in hand
Chatting to the worm.
Mr Dreadlock made a move
Waving a mango to share.
Fisherman dug his yellow teeth in the ripe mango
Hell, he'll finish it!
Mr. Dreadlock did not mind.
He lit a cigar,
And sat next to the brother found.
Speech was in the waves that rose to kiss their feet
The sweeping tide uniting their souls
Two worlds thawed into one.
At dusk's late hour,
Dreadlock hugged Fisherman
Like he'd miss him all his life
First it seemed odd
No word passed between them,
No common language
Why would they be close?
But why would it be wrong?
There,
On the rock
Was brotherhood utmost.

*

**Colours**

You spelt out the colours:
White for wholeness
Grey for growth
And Lilac for love
Where was sunshine?
A thick yellow,
And where was red?
Screaming flames
Surely lush green should be for growth!
Grey would never do among my colours!

But then,
Life in its tempest displayed greyness
And so did we grow
Our best time to learn.

And Lilac for love?
It's a pale colour that lost a purple tint!
'If you don't keep light hues for want of a deeper shade
Life itself begins to fade.'

And white for wholeness?
'It is collective,
For all the colours that create wonders and yet can't be seen
White covers them all.'

Our lives continually unfold in texture
No colours are missing.

'I see'

'You do?'

Oh, to be a child again,
And learn more than the colours…

*

**Love**

Love is real,
Love is tangible
Whoever said love was untouchable
Must have missed the boat.

Love is held,
Love is seen
Whoever said love was steam
Surely missed the boat.

Love is marble,
Sturdy oak
Whoever said love was weak
Missed the boat.

Love is material,
You can stroke and feel
Whoever said love was wacky
Did miss the boat.

\*

**The Cross**

I paused today,
When I saw the sign
That cancelled my past.

I searched my soul the day,
When I beheld the icon
That promised a pristine start.

I fell on my knees today,
When I touched the image
That held my life in balance.

I wept today,
When I embraced the piece of wood
That gave life.

*

## Another Chance

A heart screams pain,
Love and loss
What's there to gain?
A broken life at most.

Human tenderness cropped
Body injected with icicles
Turned to frost.

A voice tells a story,
And speaks restoration:
'Don't focus on the iceberg,
Your place is in the rainbow
You must Live and Love again'

Can there be a tree
Where now lay ashes and stumps?

It's not easier than before
Desert days are hot and arid
Wintry nights bitter and arctic.

'Do not listen to distractions'
Courage insists

You cannot hear the music of the harp,
If the strings are left un-plucked

You cannot feel warmth of a fire,
If the coals are not consumed
You cannot drink juice of the grape,
If the fruit is not pressed and crushed.

Trust opens her arms
Life,
Promises that beckon,
The heart with fractures
Welcomes the sunshine.

\*

**Perhaps**

Perhaps,
I shall leave the door wide open
For him to walk right through.

Perhaps,
I shall hear him whistle
Even if it's just in my dreams.

Perhaps,
I shall listen to the familiar tune
With traces of comfort.

Perhaps,
I shall watch him stagger into my kitchen and implore;
'Will you please make me a cup of coffee?'

*

## Biologically Complicated

He says I am the bridge of his nose
A passage that carries air to his lungs.

He says I am the pupil of his eye
A guide to paths un-trodden before.

He says I am the gum of his teeth
The reason he's not ashamed to smile.

He says I am the crook of his elbow
Without me his sinews don't flex.

He says I am the cap of his knee
That walks him across the expanse of love-land.

This evening at the cinema,
I watched him kiss a girl deep to deep
I broke the bridge of his nose
And left without respiration.

*

## Solo Blues

Rain pelts at my window like a scratching ghost
My heart catches a chill
Balls of ice squeeze through my skin
Dampening my soul.
The kettle dances on hot coal
Mocha coffee
The hot water scalds my fingers
The coffee burns my tongue.
Perhaps I should read an engaging memoir
Way down the forth page of 'Angela's Ashes,'
Empty me-thoughts remain.
The book slips through my hands and drops to the floor
'Get John Denver singing,'
The strum of his dear old guitar brings wetness to my eyes
I become the Falling Leaves in his song
I open the door to escape
The cold December wind whips me in the face
I recoil,
I am imprisoned in the five walls of my room
In the depth of within,
Cleft in a cave of daunting imagination
Lonesomeness puts his arms around me,
And I know,
I've caught solo blues.

\*

## They Asked Too Many Questions

They asked too many questions
And became victims of their own devotion
When are our husbands coming back?
Where are you taking the children?

The little ones carried lead guns on their shoulders
And dragged captains' booties.

Huts are consumed in flames.

We move our feet in the embers
'Where are the women?'
'Sshh, don't you know?
Don't ask too many questions'
'But I've asked one question?'
'Sshh, can't you see?'

We carry a little ash
For the unmarked graves
Tongues cling to our palate
Heavy with silent grief.

\*

### Gifts of who we are

Sometimes,
It's the sight of strangers holding hands
Without ever speaking a word
That restores a lost smile.

Sometimes,
It's the look of kindness in a friend's eye
Or Grandma fixing her apron strings
Announcing dinner is ready.

Sometimes,
It's hearing words of welcome
Saying 'I'll pray for you'
Whispering 'bless you',
That removes the pain.

Sometimes,
It's the mundane inquiries that make us human
'Would you like a drink?'
'Here, have a hug,
And a cup of good coffee.'

Sometimes,
It's the little things we do
And then realize oh, there are no little things
Someone to whisper 'remember me'
Hey, would you call such a little thing?
Or someone mentioning your name,
Those are the gifts of who we are.

\*

## After the Tsunami

Pain is in the swollen silence
That comes after watching
The broadcast news-
Laughter fades,
Deep calls to deep of every nation
Eyes search for a place,
To lay down the sorrow.

Trapped in a web of tangled emotions,
Wordless wounds fester,
We stand on the banks and exhume the debris
Remembrance is nothing but this crumbled pile.

We did not notice how it started,
Waves that were callous,
Gathered their force and ripped us apart
Wails of a thousand voices echo:
Prove that God is there, attest to his care!

We are stripped of all answers.

Tears happen,
Hearts splinter
Loneliness and terror,
Make their visitation known
This is what it means;
To hold infinity in a grain of sand,

To watch leaves blown by wind fall to the ground
We too, are severed by the seasons' change,
The price of memory crippled by loss.

The sky wears a clock of bereavement
The moon is sombre stricken,
We hung between despair and brokenness
Strands of grief weave us together
We are knotted into a ball of mourning
Wrapped in heartache's arms
Only blinding faith and generous hands sustains us,
In the wake of Tsunami.

*

## Unspoken

A golden sun sets against a purple sky
Silvery-white clouds wrap the day
Night arrives, pure and enchanting
A few metres away from his table,
She's sipping white wine.
He's touching a cold beer, watches her
Soft speakers near-by hum When I am 64
She looks up and meets his gaze,
He smiles
She returns the smile,
Their eyes embrace
No words pass between them.
Years later,
When she's older and losing her hair
And he's a grandfather wasting away
They still remember no love greater than
The unspoken,
Carried in the warmness of their eyes.

\*

**Poem for Betty Kituyi**

*Cleaning*

Today,
I dusted my shelves
And polished the souvenirs I cherish
My eyes clung to the photo frame
But, but
I had cleaned that experience out of my life
My heart repeated a long-forgotten performance
Joy.
Love.
Pain.
Hope.
I look at him absorbingly, at us
The passing of time only legalises facts
'We never stop loving the people we once loved loudly'
I pin my ears to my heart
A silent echo, a silent love sleeps in the deep
Is he well, where is he?
Stashed memories spring out of chambers
'We love silently the people we once loved loudly'
I wipe my shelves,
The shelves of memory I cannot clean.

\*

## Will We?

Will we hold our hands I pray,
When we fail to see the way?

Will you leave me alone to roam,
Or you'll come and take me home?

Will we smile and dance and rap,
Or brood and feel we're in a trap?

Will we to the altar run today,
Or consider another day?

Will we live by time and tide,
In the evenings sit by the fire-side?

Will our deeds be a heroic story,
Or we shall be forever sorry?

Will we love and stay together,
Even in tempestuous weather?

Will we live to tell the tale,
Or we shall be lost in the gale?

*

## A Cup of Coffee

Exhausted,
Spent,
Leaning against a white-washed wall
Waiting for a cup of coffee.

Red-wine eyes skirt here, there
Transmitting sleepless nights.
The coffee comes
The waitress smiles.

He examines the ten thousand shillings note
Smells the cappuccino.
On his way out of the café
He knocks his foot against the door.

'Hey, here!'
The waitress runs after him with his balance
He looks at the coins
And drops them in his trousers' pocket.

As soon as he reaches outside,
A young ruffian rushes in
He grins to find the untouched cappuccino
And gives thanks; 'A cup of coffee is never wasted.'

\*

# Poems of Identity and Renunciation

**I Know who You Are**

You promise air
With your belly full of swine
That you will sign a cheque and pay my school fees,
And build a cottage for my mother,
While your eyes squirm here, there,
Your ear to the door,
Your fear of getting caught
As your hands forcefully fondle my young chest.
I know who you are Sir,
Don't think me blind
I may be dropping out of school soon,
But not out of my senses
I know who you are Mister,
You are a balloon and with my teeny pin,
I will expose you!

*

## I Will Be

I am the inch pin of your memory
Without me you cannot be
You may deny me existence
And shut me in your backyard
Still,
I'll be.

You may steal from me motherhood
Lie that I am not the woman of your children
You may spray dirt on my face
To cover your own shame
Still,
I'll be.

I have lived a thousand times
I'll live again
I've made a pact with destiny
Nothing you do can weaken me
I will be.

Strike me,
Inflict pain
Still,
I'll be

Without me you cannot be.

*

**You Tell Us**

You tell us to be daring
Life is all about courage
When we advance to conquer,
You scream; what craziness is this?

You tell us to seize the moment
Fortune is not served in the market place
When we plunge in the pool of risk
You despise our efforts.

You tell us to be hawks
The world is managed by sharks
When we soar skywards
You ask; what kind of women are these?

*

**I Wasn't Born a Woman**

I wasn't born a woman
My sister said.
I got blisters when I washed clothes
And burnt my hands when I ironed.
Lifting the big family aluminium,
Hot water often scalded my fingers.
When I cut the onions,
They went direct into my eyes,
Giving me a running nose.
When I chopped the cabbage,
The knife often missed the intended target,
And got my flesh.

When I went to school,
My brilliance glowed like the sun
The teachers concluded:
I should have been male.
Throughout my career years,
I've soared through promotions
In councils and round table meetings
My views are priority.
Recently there was a debate
Who should represent the state round the globe
My name shone like quick silver.
And when I won the bid,
To provide consultancy away from home
People exclaimed:
She wasn't born a woman!

Now that I'm off to the Congress
To spin with computers
My mother tries to make me swear
That upon return, I should settle like a woman.
But Father says: 'To the bridge dear girl,
 Go ahead and make my dreams come true!'
Well, for sure I know nothing about his dreams.
But won't someone kindly tell me what it is to be a woman?

\*

## That Old Man on a Bench In a Park

I see him from the tall eucalyptus trees
With frail hands he waves off falling leaves
Like they're mosquitoes come to suck his blood.
Why does he sit here all day long, alone?
'He's a cynic' the scoffers say.
'He's looking for loopholes in the sun.'

The old man has his eyes to the open sky
Like some angel up there is painting his face
Sometimes he smiles,
Sometimes there's an echo of loud laughter
And a grin of forgetfulness
The world turns:
No one knows how long he's been there
Has he got a name?
He carries a small sisal sac containing his lunch
Does he live alone, has he got a home?
We make guesses about him,
We do not approach him,
Keep off the personal-

Now the old man has his head in his hands
That's the way he takes his nap
His frame wrapped in a black overcoat
A long checked umbrella folded by his side
Perhaps he's a saint in a pilgrims park
And that bench his resting plank.

\*

## Some Men Find it Hard to Complete Sentences

He's sheltered black smudges in the nook of his gaze
He holds a pair of broken life in the sad shade of his eyes.
A belt of bruised reed coupled in the rings of his trousers
A forlorn look, a sight of grief with sticks climbing a
        lonely hill
His feeble knees give way,
There's a fall.
Those passing-by ask why a man like him should be so
        weak
The laughter of sadness in his eyes drops,
And releases a sudden tale
Tears run generously,
The silence of his voice speaks louder:
The echo of the unspoken word grips the air
A passage of time and his tongue tries:
So-me s-o-m-e-ti-me-s,
So-so-me men f-f-find it, hard t-t-to-co-mplete
        se-nte-nce-s
It's not funny to see him stammer
If he can simply utter a word, it's human enough-
The sigh from his chest is a sonorous reverberation,
The black smudges under his eyes begin to disappear,
The isolation of his ears from other facial features lift
        up the sound
The boom of loss, despair, un-love, goodbye, amnesia,
        contrition

A long index of infamous last words
The passers-by leave him alone
There's no comfort in a lost voice.
In the ultimate,
He pokes the reservoir of inner courage
And picks up the broken fabrics to weave himself again
Into a tapestry that those passing by won't leave alone.

*

**Forgotten**

In a corner,
In a pot obscured from sunshine,
A weeping dying rose I see.

Light!
I cry out.

In an oak tree,
In a forest ridden with hail,
A crippled freezing bird I notice.

Ladder,
I scream.

In a swamp,
Forgotten by rain,
A bruised drying reed I find.

Goodness!
What shall be saved?

Beginning of creation,
And I to witness their end-
I retreat into my self,
Feeling the pain of dying in existence.

\*

## At the Inauguration of a Pauper

The handcuffed man
Sat poised,
To answer the questions.
The first interviewer opened his book
Out of his lips sauntered the words:
Were you born a pauper?
yes, truly
What's there to show?
my father and mother, they live from hand to
mouth
i never saw a blackboard.
And you speak standard English?
i picked it from the streets
What qualifies you a pauper now?
staying on the street, having no wife, no home,
privileges i can't afford so i remain a pauper.
The rest are satisfied with pauper's explanation
They write in their big books:
Pauper on Wilson Street:
No wife, no property, no inheritance, no nothing.

The pauper survives the graduated tax.

*

## Child of the Universe

Why do you believe a lie
That you are Third World?
Whoever told you,
We have more worlds than one?

Why do you trade with deception
That you are a production mistake,
Biological accident,
Undesired?

Child of the Universe,
Many years spent,
With your resilient self
You still don't know who you are?

*

## Life

Wintry weather plasters the sun
And dribbles icicles on a fragile heart
A scary lonely presence
Shatters smiles.
An eerie sensation
Resides around people of every hue.
Fires of youth are gone with earnest feelings
Hollow laughter escorts the mute cry
Grinning faces
Behind empty coffee cups.
Billows of cigarette smoke
Motion images
Industrial noises
Oh, life!

\*

## Bust Cisterns

As if the clouds wear a shroud of misery
We do not see the promised sun

Empty eyes of children ask us why

Night brings the moon stricken with sadness
And grief swells in our hearts
Gunshots declare the dirge
Terror claims us
Wails of a thousand widows tear the environs
Rivers of blood
Congeal in thick black clots

Empty eyes of children ask us why

'Christ save us!
Children of barrenness'

We are much on our knees
Creeping where we ought to run

Utterance brings us hope
And song in the night

In our dreams is the hope of tomorrow

We are bruised reeds,

Refusing to be broken

Smoking flax,
That is not put out

We are struck but not destroyed,
Living our sorrow like shining armour

Wind stirs,
Our voices rise against a frightening sky

In our dreams is the hope of tomorrow

We are not afraid anymore
We make crowns where there are no jewels
And watch dandelions bloom upon a deserted path
There are no herds in our fathers' kraals
Flocks are cut from the fold
The fields yield no fruit
We quench our thirst from bust cisterns.

And we survive,
Fighting still.

*

**Borderless Africa**

He says,
We are a continuous stream,
Not a classification
There isn't a you, me or the other,
We are us.

Borderless Africa
Borderless Africa.

They say,
Before time began
We were,
Now the cord is broken,
Dismembered from the source.

Borderless Africa,
Borderless Africa,
Flow,
Connect us again
We cry for you.

\*

## Baggage

Memories packed in one old bag,
Stubbornly jump out
To be tucked in, again.

The milk of tenderness
Spills from unzipped corner
To soak shoulders.

Wounds surface from the deep
There's hardly strength
To summon winds of forgetfulness

Pain makes her dwelling among the familiar
Refusing to whisper goodbye.

*

**Gaza**

A frail woman who has forgotten the smile of gods
Protests against soldiers stamping their feet,
Marching to bondage.
This is our land,
Give us our Gaza!
Her shouts fall upon dead hearts of captors
Her mouth sags and drools
Releasing a tale of detention in old age
Infancy
Failed youth
She falls to the ground
Dies holding a lump of soil
A piece of her Gaza.

\*

## Do not Look for Me Among the Broken Pots

Do not look for me among the broken pots:
My place is in the skies
Long ago I chose the rainbow for my skin,
And lightness for my soul

I am the torch of a million stars,
The radiance in your dreams.

Do not look for me among the ruined huts
My seat is at the Chief's table:
Elected before time began
Brother, sister, do not weep

I am the fortified path,
That bears your footprints home.

*

**Becoming gods**

Hands joined,
We leave the clefts,
To make our own dwelling on the heights.
I manage to nest among the stars,
While he builds a bridge from Jupiter to the Sun
Finally we are gods!
The kites fly slightly below us,
We boast in our immortality
I do not notice worms eating through my nest,
He does not see the termites destroying the bridge,
Bit by bit.
We crush to the ground,
Wingless.
We gather feathers of our pride
And retrace our steps to the rock
How did we deceive ourselves we would be,
Without Him who makes us be?

*

**Oneness**

I love the music of his pipe:
To lie down at his feet,
And feel the deep of his eyes
Upon me.

I drink of his wine, refined
And clothe in his wool, warm
He cushions me to his bosom,
Deep rivers of calm encircle me.

I hear a song of them that triumph,
A shout of them that feast,
The harpers of heaven are here,
The music of his saints.

*

## Picture Bazaar

I see their faces on the wall,
Quill pens stuck in their breast pockets.
Their eyes much alive pore into my soul
For clues of allegiance.
I edge back in shame.
I turn to walk away,
Too late.
Their eyes remain on me.
Hesitantly, I face them.
I am moving through continents
Centuries, face-scapes
Like fast forward slides
There's Whitman, Dickinson
Hemingway, Woolf, Nietzsche,
Pound, Frost, Tolstoy, Roy,
Soyinka, Bitek, Sindiwe, Ishiguro…
Continuing presences
Joy in brief,
Minds spattered with spots of depression
I want to touch them,
Feel them,
Smell them.
Mixed genres of voices leap from the walls
To walk in the shade of their scripts
Resisting death.
Their faces stare at me.
'I seek your muse,' words roll off my tongue.

And they whisper:
'Are you ready to forsake all but the creative words,
Follow our solitary path like a signal from the gods?'
The pictures shine in laureate armour.
Changed by their own devotion,
This time I know,
I must follow and stand out with them.

\*

www.ingramcontent.com/pod-product-compliance
Lightning Source LLC
Chambersburg PA
CBHW020014050426
42450CB00005B/471

*9 7 8 1 8 5 6 5 7 1 0 2 9 *